Gathering Around the Table

Children and Communion

Published by the Baptist Union of Great Britain
The Baptist Union of Great Britain
Baptist House, 129 Broadway, Didcot
Oxfordshire, OX11 8RT, United Kingdom
www.baptist.org.uk

**BAPTISTS
TOGETHER**

This book was compiled by the Faith and Unity Department of the Baptist Union of
Great Britain, with particular thanks for the work of Anthony Clarke,
Andy Goodliff and Graham Sparkes.

British Library cataloguing in Publication Data
Data Available
ISBN 978-0-901472-51-9

Contents

Introduction

It is Easter Sunday morning and your church has met together for a special early morning breakfast and communion to begin the celebration of Jesus' resurrection. There are about 50 people present of varying ages. While the smell of coffee and sausages waft through from the kitchen the congregation are sitting around tables formed into a big rectangle, laid for breakfast. They have sung and prayed and heard read again the encounter between the risen Jesus and the disciples early in the morning after they had been fishing for the night. Before they echoed Jesus' words to "come and have breakfast", the minister took a loaf of bread and a cup of wine and offered it to the congregation. As the bread begins to be passed around, Luke, who is eight, whispers in his Mum's ear, "Can I have some of the bread and wine?"

This question has been asked many times, and is being asked now with greater frequency. This in itself seems to signal a change in Baptist churches over recent decades. Some of us may remember, as children, being ushered out of church when it was about to be communion – it was thought that this was not a suitable occasion for children. But the increasing desire within churches to worship as a whole family and the willingness of churches to experiment, such as with a breakfast communion, means that there are many more occasions when children will ask to be included. Their request may arise from a whole variety of reasons and motives. How would we respond if we were asked? How should we respond as a church?

These are the kind of questions which this study will seek to address. It is not a simple matter, but it raises many significant questions. It asks us to think about the nature of the church as a gathered company of believers and the meaning of communion as part of this church's worship. It also raises the question of how 'childhood' is understood and respected in the twenty-first century in the light of recent research. These are questions which, it has to be admitted, Baptists have yet to resolve satisfactorily.

They are also not questions which Baptists are asking alone, although our understanding of church and baptism mean that they will be focussed in particular and unique ways for us. Other denominations are also wrestling with the same developments in the understanding of children and questioning the ways that children are included in their worship and church life.

One of the significant changes in recent years has been the increasing mobility of people, not just geographically but between different church traditions. As individuals and families move and settle in a new church, it may be because of its geographical proximity, or its style of worship, or its youth work or its friendly welcome regardless of its 'label'. Consequently even the 'average Baptist church' will count within its number those who have followed the Baptist route of Infant Presentation, Believer's Baptism and reception into church membership, as well as those who were baptised as infants, confirmed and placed upon an electoral roll - with a host of variations between and beyond those positions. They may bring with them different understandings of ministry and worship, and the responsibility of congregational members in the ordering and government of the church. As Baptist churches wrestle with questions of children and communion they are often doing so with this kind of mixed congregation. For some, who work and worship in Local Ecumenical Partnerships, these diverse traditions will come together in particular and more formal ways.

This study guide is not the first attempt at a fresh understanding of the place of children in the church and their place at Communion. It has drawn upon a wealth of material provided by theologians, ministers, students and those involved in the education and nurture of children and young people. It does not set out to provide 'the Baptist position' but we do believe that there is a valid Baptist perspective to which we can contribute. Its aim is to open up discussion so that local churches may make informed decisions on the nature of Communion and the place of the child in the church's worship, fellowship and mission. It seeks to explore how children might be welcomed to this central celebration of our faith with integrity, taking seriously the nature of the meal. One thing which the study does not do is define who we mean by children, in simplistic terms of age. There are different issues relating to children of different ages, but we have not tried to separate them here into different age groups. We hope this will give each church freedom to look at the whole subject in a way that is appropriate to their own context.

The material can be divided into three parts. The first, studies 1-3, explores the nature of communion and what it means for us in the light of the ministry of Jesus and the experiences of the Church at Corinth. The second, studies 4 and 5, contains a brief summary of recent thought on the place of the child in church and society. The final study then seeks to bring these two streams of thought together and gives some examples of what churches might do in practice.

Each study begins with several pages of reflection on the issues, of Scripture, theology and contemporary understandings. Then there is a series of questions or exercises to help a group work through these issues. At the end of each section is an exercise in which to involve children. It is vital, especially in the light of some of the theology expressed in these chapters, that we do not simply come to a decision that is 'imposed' on children, but that we hear their voices as well. There will be many other ways of enabling this to happen, and each congregation will be in a position to decide how best to engage their own children, but we suggest here some ideas which could be part of that conversation. We do this in the hope that wherever these questions are considered the voices of children are welcomed and affirmed.

We hope that you will use the material as best suits you, which may mean looking at just some of the questions here and/or adding others you think would be helpful. If you are using it as the basis of a group study over several weeks, it would be best if all the members could read the pages of reflection for that study beforehand and come ready to work through the issues. Take as long as you like over each section. You may wish to spend more than one week's meeting on one or even over-run from one into the next.

Study One
Around the Table with Jesus

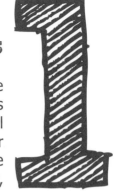

Among the various names or titles given to the service of communion, most popular among Baptists has been 'The Lord's Supper'. This is a very helpful description. It reminds us that we do not gather around the table of the church but the table of the Lord, that we share a meal in which we believe that, though prepared and led by different people, Jesus is the host. Any attempt to think about communion, therefore, must begin with Jesus. A key part of this will be thinking about the Last Supper which Jesus shared with his disciples. This time was such an influence on the development of communion within the early church. But this, of course, was not the only meal that Jesus shared with his disciples, with the crowds and even with his opponents. Meals were a central part of Jesus' ministry and also feature significantly in his teaching. We begin, then, by thinking about sitting at the table with Jesus.

Table Fellowship

There are a number of passages in the Gospels that are concerned with shared meals. Two particular kinds of story can be identified. First there are those accounts of Jesus at table with others, either as host or guest, which are normally used by the Gospel writers to draw attention to the company that Jesus kept. Second, there are those accounts which also centre around table-fellowship, but in which some have seen elements that either prefigure or echo the meal at the Last Supper.

The first group would include the dinner at Levi's, or Matthew's, house (Matt 9:9-13; Lk 5:27-32), an evening with Simon the Pharisee (Lk 7:36-50), a Sabbath meal with another Pharisee (Lk 14:1-14), Zacchaeus (Lk 19:1-10), the wedding at Cana (Jn 2:1-11) and the Samaritan woman at the well (Jn 4:1-26). In some the context clearly involved those on the fringes of society, who act as the host. So Jesus responds to an invitation from Levi, invites himself to Zacchaeus' house and requests water from the Samaritan woman. In a clear and noted distinction from the expected behaviour Jesus refuses to construct fences around his table-fellowship. In the two occasions when Luke records Jesus accepting invitations from a Pharisee, the point drawn out in the Gospel explicitly contrasts the attitude of Jesus with that of his host. In Luke 7:36-50 Simon is presented as someone who stands aloof from Jesus, despite the normal customs of hospitality, and pointedly separate from the woman who enters his house, who herself performs the duties of the host. Jesus in an enacted and spoken parable, welcomes and willingly receives the hospitality which the woman has to offer and in return speaks words of grace. In Luke 14:1-14, after a further invitation and further disruption, controversy is initiated by healing on the Sabbath. But rather than explore this contentious issue the dialogue quickly moves on to the customs of table fellowship, first in respect of the honoured seats and then in respect of the invitation list. We see in Jesus someone who deliberately dismantles those fences erected by religious tradition.

> **Jesus refuses to construct fences around his table-fellowship**

Jesus' willingness to eat with those rejected by other parts of society, 'tax-collectors and sinners', seems to have been one of the reasons why Jesus provoked opposition. Luke introduces the three parables of the lost sheep, coin and son, with the grumbling of the Pharisees that Jesus 'welcomes sinners and eats with them'. But, if we were to take the encounter with Zacchaeus as an example, Jesus does not stop with an act of welcome. Jesus initiates the conversation and invites himself to Zacchaeus' house – this act of grace finds a response in Zacchaeus' welcome. But the climax of the story is Zacchaeus' repentance, shown in the financial restoration offered. Grace, welcome and repentance all combine together in this one episode. But what is the relationship between grace and repentance? The implication of this passage seems to be that repentance is the response to grace and fellowship rather than a necessary condition for it to happen. This seems to be a stress in Luke's Gospel, for it was with 'sinners' that Jesus ate. The challenge to repentance and change is central to the ministry of Jesus, but we must wrestle with how this relates to Jesus' gracious initiative in sharing meals with all.

The second group of narratives centre upon the feeding of the 5000 (Matt 14: 13-21; Mk 6:30-44; Lk 9:10-17; Jn 6:1-15), and 4000 (Matt 15:32-9; Mk 8:1-13), the post-resurrection meal with the two disciples at Emmaus (Lk.24:13-35), and the post-resurrection breakfast on the beach (Jn 21:1-14). There are divided opinions as to whether in these meals there are deliberate echoes of the Last Supper and Lord's Supper. Jesus' actions in taking, blessing, breaking and sharing the bread are the same actions as at the Last Supper, so the parallel is clear, but they are also the familiar and everyday actions of any meal. The question is whether or not the Gospel writers might intend us to make that kind of connection. This is most acute in John's account of the feeding of the 5000, particularly because there is no account of the Last Supper in John's Gospel. Yet after relating the feeding of the 5000, as in the other Gospels, Jesus engages the crowd about what they had experienced. He speaks to them about being the bread of life who has come down from heaven (6:35, 51) and challenges the crowd that 'unless you eat the flesh of the Son of God and drink his blood you have no life in you' (6:53). This has led some commentators to suggest that John has deliberately portrayed the feeding of the 5000 as like the Last Supper, but with a very different group of people – the whole crowd rather than just the few disciples.

The Last Supper

Not only does the Last Supper fit into this general pattern of the Gospels in which meals were important, but it was a significant meal for the Jewish people. At the Last Supper the disciples share the traditional Jewish Passover meal which Jesus filled with new significance. Indeed many churches now would have either a Passover meal on Maundy Thursday evening or a communion service on that day shaped more closely by that meal. While there are clearly differences between the Passover and the Lord's Supper, between the Jews as a whole nation and the Church, this connection between Lord's Supper and Passover is significant in a number of ways. It helps shape the way we understand the significance of what we are doing to remember Jesus' death, for here was God's occasion of salvation, so that Jesus' death is 'for us'. It could shape the way we understand the language which has often proved to be difficult, 'This is my body', for at Passover various objects were on the table and the host would explain them by saying 'this is...' It might also shape the answer we give to who should gather at the table, for the Passover was a feast for all the family regardless of age, and also one in which strangers and guest were made particularly welcome.

If we look at how the Gospels tell this story, Matthew, Mark and Luke (the three 'synoptic' Gospels) all frame the sharing of bread and wine in some way with the betrayal and denial of Jesus. This does more than set it in a historical context.

Jesus quite deliberately shares this last supper at which he encourages his friends to continue to celebrate his transforming presence in bread and wine with those he knows will betray and deny him; they are included to the last. Such framing of the meal was clearly an early part of the church's tradition, for Paul also recalls that these events happened not simply on the night before he died, but on the night when he was betrayed. Those who were his friends and disciples and had followed him from the beginning have now let him down. Luke frames the meal not only with the thoughts and actions of Peter and Judas, but also with the dispute about greatness that engulfs the whole group. The Last Supper then is an occasion of challenge and a moment of grace, where in the midst of human sin and brokenness Jesus offers himself. This asks of us the same questions about the way that repentance might follow on from, and be brought about by, the prior offer of grace.

The Great Banquet

Building on the importance of actual meals, Jesus also uses the meal table as a significant part of his teaching, in particular in his parables of a future heavenly banquet (Matt 22:1-14; Lk 14:15-24). Such teaching is not new, but is also an Old Testament picture, perhaps being seen most clearly in Isaiah 25:6-9:

'On this mountain the Lord Almighty will prepare a feast of rich food for all peoples, a banquet of aged wine – the best of meats and finest of wines. On this mountain he will destroy the shroud that enfolds all peoples, the sheet that covers all nations; he will swallow up death for ever.'

Not only does Isaiah point to the future with God by using this image of a feast, it is also part of the wrestling within the Old Testament as to the part the Gentiles would play in this future. Here Isaiah looks to a time when all peoples and all nations would be included. Jesus' parable continues to deal with this same question of inclusion. The parables stress different things in the two Gospels. Matthew has a greater emphasis on judgment, and seems to have in his mind the ongoing struggles between the Synagogue and the Church (many of whom were Jews). While in Luke's Gospel the parable is spoken in the house of a prominent Pharisee, and the details suggest that it was some kind of banquet or celebratory meal in the home of a wealthy individual. The parable then clearly reflects the setting and emphasises Jesus' preceding comments about choosing the lowest places at the meal, clearly a response to the jockeying for position that he has witnessed.

The parable itself is in response to the declaration that whoever eats at the feast in the kingdom of God is blessed. Whereas the parable does have echoes of this great banquet, at this first level Jesus' response to the outburst is to confront his fellow diners, whom we can assume were all of this elevated social status. What matters is not some pious longing for the future banquet but radically different social behaviour in the present. In Luke's account of the parable, the host responds to the social snub of rejection by breaking apart the whole social system of inviting to dinner people who were the same social status as you were, and instead inviting those who could not come. The excluded had to be compelled to come in, because the social division was so entrenched they simply could not imagine such an invitation. This then at one level is a parable about table fellowship and the company we keep in the here and now. It reflects Jesus' own practice and prepares the way for the muttered comment in 15:2, which introduces the parables of the lost sheep, coin and son, that 'This man welcomes sinners and eats with them.'

But the parable also works at another level, seen in the pious outburst about the messianic banquet, for Jesus addresses those invited to this banquet as well. We might be left with the sense that the rich have the invitation first and the poor are invited as something of an afterthought when the rich had declined the invitation. This would be to push the parable too far. Jesus speaks in this way to address the social issues around him. But there is also the suggestion that when the owner sends his slave 'outside' this is a symbolic reference to the Gentiles, noting that in the parable the command is given but not yet acted upon. In this way the parable echoes the gracious promise of Isaiah 25 and echoes the concern for the Gentiles found elsewhere in this Gospel.

> **the parable offers an image and a challenge of grace – the graciousness of God who invites all to the messianic banquet**

So at both levels, the parable offers an image and a challenge of grace – the graciousness of God who invites all to the messianic banquet and the call to such gracious living in the here and now. The parable also combines the two levels of the 'here and now' and the 'future feast', it does so in such a way that the future messianic banquet shapes the way we live and act in the present that the grace implicit in such an invitation might be the mark of our own table fellowship in the here and now.

Conclusion

So we are left with a number of issues and questions that demand our response.

How much should the rest of the Gospel material about Jesus' practice of table fellowship influence our decisions about who should be welcome to the Lord's Table today?

How much should the background of the Last Supper as a Passover meal influence our decisions about who should be welcome to the Lord's Table today?

Does the way that Jesus confronted the religious practice of social exclusion need to challenge the way we are, as church today, including communion?

There are, of course, significant differences between the actual meals that Jesus shared with many people and the service of the Lord's Supper. These differences themselves might ask questions of the way we have come to celebrate Communion. Instinctively we tend to look to Paul's account of Communion in 1 Corinthians 11 (which we will discuss in the next chapter), but if it is the Lord's Supper, then the whole ministry of Jesus as recorded in the Gospels should help shape the way we think about Communion. In particular, we have discussed the challenge inherent in the welcome Jesus gave to and received from 'sinners'. What do we expect before someone comes to share at the Lord's Table and what do we look for as a response?

For study and discussion

- The Introduction began with a true story of an Easter morning breakfast and communion. If you were in that service and 'Luke' whispered in your ear, how would you respond (you only have 30 seconds before the plate with the bread is passed to you)?

- How we answer the above question is important, not because it is right or wrong, but because it suggests how we instinctively react to the question of children and communion. Take a few minutes to think and talk together about the reasons for your instinctive response. What might have shaped the way you think so that you respond in this way?

- If you could stop time, and instead of 30 seconds you had a few hours or days to think about your answer, what questions would be important for you to think about before you give your answer? (Some of these will probably come up in later studies so you don't need to answer them all now!)

- Read Luke 19:1-10. This account weaves together repentance, faith and sharing a meal with Jesus. Does a passage like this have any contribution to how we understand the Lord's Supper in the church? If so, what?

- Read John 6:1-15, 25-59. Remember that John's Gospel does not have an account of the Last Supper meal; instead John records Jesus washing the disciples' feet. Some have suggested that this chapter has the same function, and hints throughout to what the church came to know as the Lord's Supper. What evidence can you find in the passage for this?

- Do you feel that John is deliberately thinking about the Lord's Supper in this passage? What might the significance of this be?

- The last meal that Jesus shared with his disciples was the Passover. This was, and is, an important occasion for Jewish people at which all the family gather. Its annual repetition is a way in which the faith and understanding of the religious community is nurtured. Recognising the differences between the Passover and the Lord's Supper, could the Lord's Supper also be a place where the faith of all is nurtured? How might this be accomplished?

- The Gospels show us how Jesus welcomed and ate with the marginalised. Should we today, at the Lord's Supper, try and break down barriers and welcome the marginalised, or should we set boundaries on who should be welcome? How would you answer the person who said, 'Jesus welcomed everyone – so should we'? Where do you think boundaries should be drawn?

- Think back to your answer to the first question. Has the study and discussion helped you to understand more clearly the reasons behind your instinctive decision or has it made you think in new ways?

Engaging Children

Tell the following story:

Ellie was very excited. It was only three weeks to her birthday. She had been talking with her Mum and Dad for a while about what kind of party she should have. They had decided on a swimming party, followed by tea and a birthday cake. Ellie's Mum had booked the local swimming pool for the Saturday afternoon, just after her birthday. Now they were writing the invitations. Mum said that she could invite 15 friends, as well as her brother and sister and two cousins. Ellie had been writing a list of names, but there were more than 20 friends on her list. 'Can I have more than 15?', she asked her Mum. 'No', her Mum replied, 'because the Swimming Pool have said that there can only be 20 children altogether'. 'Oh, no', thought Ellie, 'what shall I do? How do I decide which people to invite and which ones to leave out?'

Invite the children to respond to the story. What might the different people have felt? How does it make connections to their own experiences?

From this basis ask the children how they understand the invitation of God and how they have experienced that being expressed in and through the church.

Tell them about the way Jesus tried to share meals with everyone, and the stories he told about everyone being invited by God.

14

Study Two
Around the Table in Corinth

Although the three synoptic Gospels give us an account of the Last Supper, the only extended discussion on the Lord's Supper in the New Testament comes in a letter Paul wrote to the Church at Corinth (1 Cor 11:17-34). The reason Paul chooses to write about communion is that some people in the church in Corinth were behaving at it in a way which the apostle Paul regarded as seriously reprehensible. The 'words of institution' which are used in most churches when the Lord's Supper is celebrated today come from this passage (verses 23-26), but most people know little about their context. At best there is a vague awareness that the Corinthians were misbehaving in some way, but there is little understanding of just what it was about their behaviour that concerned Paul so much that he wrote the rather harsh words of verses 27-29. If we are to understand how Paul's comments will be relevant for us today, then we must understand what led him to speak so forcefully.

The problem - social divisiveness

To begin to appreciate that, we must recognise that in Paul's day the Lord's Supper was part of an actual meal eaten by the community in a private home, with one of the wealthier members of the church hosting it. Archaeological excavations of 1st century AD houses, including one at Corinth, combined with descriptions from classical writers of how people entertained guests, give helpful light on what Paul says here. The dining room (the *triclinium*) in these houses was quite small. At formal meals the guests reclined on couches, and it is estimated that no more than 9-12 people could be entertained in the dining room. Outside the dining room was a larger reception hall (the *atrium*) which could hold about 30-50 people if they sat rather than reclined. The normal practice at a large meal was for the host to eat in the dining room with a few select guests, to whom he wanted to show particular honour. By entertaining them he also boosted his own status. These guests were given better, and more plentiful, food than those dining in the hall. Against this background we can make good sense of what Paul says about how some in Corinth were behaving.

Paul is addressing those who are wealthy — those who have houses (11:22, 34) and plenty of food (11:21). Such people would have been a minority in the church (1:26). These wealthy members were hosting the Lord's Supper but treating it like one of their normal social dinners as an opportunity to flaunt their social status by the way they conducted the meal. So Paul stresses that it is not the *Lord's* supper that they are eating, but 'each of you goes ahead with your *own* supper'. The way many English versions translate the first part of verse 21 suggests that the better off, who did not have to worry about a long day's manual work, are going ahead and eating their meal before the less fortunate have even arrived. However, the word Paul uses here can have the sense of 'consume, eat greedily', and Paul may be getting at the feasting of the select few in the dining room while the majority eating in the hall only have the 'left-overs'. But whichever situation was in Paul's mind, the 'have-nots' are treated with contempt and made to feel humiliated (which was part of the aim in an ordinary social gathering!). So, Paul's major concern is the *social divisiveness* of the way the Lord's Supper was conducted in Corinth. It was all about social status.

> **The way Paul uses the word for 'come together' is important**

The main issue for Paul is social divisiveness. He has provided a 'trailer' of 11:17-34 in 10:16-17 where he stresses that sharing the 'one bread' should be an expression of the fact that Christians 'who are many are one body'. The way Paul uses the word for 'come together' in 11:17-34 is important. He uses it five times (11:17,18,20,33,34). It's not just about meeting. It should be an expression of genuine oneness as believers in Christ. At the heart of the problem was a selfishness in which a few kept the best to themselves, rather than the gracious hospitality which so marked the ministry of Jesus.

The Last Supper and the Lord's Supper

The Corinthians seem to have prided themselves on maintaining the 'traditions' that Paul had passed on to them (11:2). So he reminds them that the Lord's Supper had its origins in what Jesus said and did at the Last Supper (11:23-26). If we look at the four different accounts of the Last Supper side by side (Matt 26:26-28; Mk 14:22-24; Lk 22:19-20; 1 Cor 11:23-25) we notice some important differences in the words that are used, and that Matthew and Mark tend to use the same language as each other, while Luke and Paul seem to have language which they share together, but different to Matthew and Mark. The significant difference is that both Paul and Luke add the words 'Do this in remembrance of me' after the 'bread saying'. Only Paul adds a further sentence after the cup saying, 'Do this, as often as you drink it, in remembrance of me'.

The fact that Paul repeats this stress on remembrance suggests that it is particularly important for him in this context. He makes clear what he meant by it when he adds to the 'tradition' the words, 'For as often as you eat this bread and drink the cup, you proclaim the Lord's death until he comes' (11:26). For a Jew like Paul 'remembering' meant more than mere information recall. It meant recalling something in order to act in the light of it. It is important that the Last Supper is usually understood to be a Passover meal (Paul alluded to this in 5:7). The purpose of that meal was to recall the deliverance of God's people from Egypt where they had been slaves, and the beginning of their journey to the promised land, so that each generation of Jews might live in the light of it. It is significant that it was in the context of a Passover meal that Jesus chose to speak of his death. His death, Paul reminds the Corinthians, was 'for you', just as the Passover lamb died for the first-born. It was a new act of deliverance which initiated a 'new covenant'. To have a covenant relationship with God means also being in a covenant relationship with God's people. This brings with it certain responsibilities to the other members of the covenant people. The character of this covenant relationship should be demonstrated by the sharing of the meal. The trouble with the way the meal was held in Corinth was that the wealthy disregarded the covenant obligations. They behaved as if Jesus' death had not brought about a decisive change in their relationship with their fellow believers — a change which Paul elsewhere says should remove ethnic, social and gender barriers (Gal 3:27-28). That is why Paul says that when they 'come together' they do not really eat 'the Lord's Supper', but simply 'your own supper' (11:20-21).

An appropriate response

We have seen how Paul is responding to a very specific situation at Corinth, and seeks to bring the Corinthians back to the essential meaning of the Lord's Supper. He then begins to suggest practical steps to remedy the situation – verse 27 begins 'therefore'. Yet the exact meaning of verses 27-34 has been hotly debated.

The first issue is what is meant by 'discerning the body', which then determines what is meant by eating and drinking 'in an unworthy manner'. Most modern commentators are agreed that the issue is not to do with there being something special or sacred about the elements of bread and wine. He sees the Lord's Supper through the lens of the Passover, in which there were other physical things full of meaning and significance, as an invitation to participate in the saving death of Jesus.

The fact that Paul says 'discerning the body' and does not add 'and blood' leads many to conclude that, given the context, he is talking about recognising the community of believers as the one body of Christ (echoing 10:16-17). On this basis, eating 'unworthily' would mean doing so in a way that provokes or sustains divisions. Others argue that since Paul speaks of 'all who eat *and drink* without discerning the body, eat *and drink* judgment against themselves' he is using 'body' as a 'shorthand' for the longer phrase, 'the body and blood of the Lord' (11:27). The repeated mention of eating the bread and drinking the cup in 11:28 is taken to support this. On this basis, eating 'unworthily' would mean doing so without proper regard to the meal being a proclamation of the Lord's death, and all that follows from that.

It would seem quite likely that Paul deliberately has both of these meanings in mind when he uses the word 'body', and seeks to hold together the body and blood of Jesus and the community of the church. Paul's concern then is about disrespecting one's fellow Christians and thereby affronting Christ by treating with contempt the meal that is meant to proclaim his

> **Paul's concern then is about disrespecting one's fellow Christians**

death. The call to self-examination, then, (11:28) has a very specific focus centred upon the way we relate to our fellow Christians as a sign of our covenant with God.

Secondly, while Paul's words about judgment in verses 29-31 need to be taken seriously today, his application of this in verse 30 should not be universalised. What he says is probably best taken as a specific word for the situation in Corinth. With prophetic insight Paul discerns a specific link between the prevalence of illness and death among the Corinthians and their actions at the Lord's Supper. In other situations the 'judgment' might be manifest in other ways. This is a matter of *discipline*, not of *condemnation*, with the implied loss of salvation. It is like a wayward child being corrected but not being thrown out of the family. What is clear is that Paul views right relationships within the church as a fundamental basis for a right participation in the Lord's Supper.

Finally, Paul rounds off his discussion of the Lord's Supper with some specific directions about their common meals. The exact meaning of verse 33 is not clear. The verb in the final clause is ambiguous. Most English translations take it in the sense 'to wait for' (its normal sense in the New Testament), in which case the wealthier Christians are being told not to get impatient and go ahead with their own meal before everyone has arrived. On the other hand, the verb can mean 'to receive, welcome'. If we take it in this sense, then Paul is calling on the wealthy Christians to break down the barrier of social inequality and to treat everyone as honoured guests, with the implication of an equal sharing of food and drink. Those who want to eat in the manner, or to the extent, to which they are accustomed should do so privately at home and not flaunt their wealth and status at the gathering for the Lord's Supper. This is something of a compromise solution, but Paul is seeking to deal with an urgent pastoral problem and so stops short of calling here for a radical social revolution.

Conclusion

These verses, especially those that speak of self-examination and divine judgment have been significant in an understanding of who should be welcome at the table. Yet, as we have seen, Paul is responding to a very specific situation, where the problem is social divisions between Christians. How then might these verses, from this context, help us reflect on who should be welcome at the table today? How does this affect whether children should be welcomed to communion?

In the light of all we have said about the context of 1 Corinthians, how should Paul's command about self-examination and eating unworthily be applied today? At different times in our past Baptist churches have taken this to mean that those who are not baptised or not church members or not clearly committed Christians, should stay away. Paul takes communion very seriously, and we should too. But what about those who are still 'on the way' to a committed relationship with Jesus Christ, who, within their understanding, will treat this meal with respect and dignity? Does this passage raise for us another question about gracious hospitality?

For study and discussion

If you truly and earnestly repent of your sins, and are in love and charity with your neighbours, and are resolved to lead a new life, following the commandments of God, and walking henceforth in his holy ways; draw near with faith, and take this sacrament to your comfort and growth in grace. Come to this sacred table, not because you must but because you may; come not to testify that you are righteous, but that you sincerely love our Lord Jesus Christ, and desire to be his true disciples; come, not because you are strong, but because you are weak; not because you have any claim on heaven's rewards, but because in your frailty and sin you stand in constant need of heaven's mercy and help.'
(From *Patterns and Prayers for Christian Worship*)

'The Table of the Lord is spread. It is for those who will come and see in broken bread and poured out wine symbols of his life shed for us on the cross and raised again on the third day. The Risen Christ is present among his people and it is here that we meet him. It is for those who know him a little and long to know him more. We invite all who are seeking him and all who are weary of their sin and doubt to come and share in the feast. If you do not feel able to take a full part, you are welcome to remain among us without receiving the bread and wine.'
(From *Patterns and Prayers for Christian Worship*)

'Brothers and sisters in Christ, it is right that we call to mind the meaning of this Supper. It is a remembrance of the sacrifice of Christ for the sin of the world; an encounter with the risen Lord; a feeding on him in faith; a communion with one another in his body, the Church; and a looking forward to the day when he will come again. Therefore, we need to come in faith, conscious of our weakness, seeking to renounce our sin, humbly putting our trust in Christ and seeking his grace.' (From *Patterns and Prayers for Christian Worship*)

'Here is the table of the Lord
we are gathered to his supper
a foretaste of things eternal.
Come, when you are fearful, to be made new in love.
Come, when you are doubtful, to be made strong in faith.
Come, when you are regretful, and be made whole.
Come, old and young,
there is room for all.'
(From *Gathering for Worship*)

- Above are some different 'invitations' to communion which might be used by the person leading the service. They help explain something about what happens in communion and also who it is intended for. Which do you like and why?

- Read 1 Corinthians 11:17-34. The setting of the church at Corinth includes difficulties about understanding what happens at communion and divisions between different members of the church. What difficulties have been raised in your church about Communion?

- The divisions appear to have been between rich and poor. What divisions do you see in your church? Is one of the contemporary divisions between adults and children?

- Verse 27 talks about recognising or discerning the body of the Lord. In the light of what has been discussed above how might you as a church today 'discern the body of the Lord', particularly when you share communion?

- Verse 28 says that we should examine ourselves before we eat? What sort of examination should this be? Does this mean that some should be discouraged from taking bread and wine? Who might these be and why?

- Verse 33 encourages the Corinthians to wait for or welcome each other. How might you put this encouragement into action in your particular congregation?

- Sharing communion is often a balance between it being an individual moment of meeting with God and a corporate celebration of our shared faith. How are both these aspects expressed in a communion service in your church? Would you want to find ways to develop the balance in a particular way?

- Think back to the 'invitations' with which we began. Which do you think might best reflect Paul's teaching as we have thought about it in this study? Thinking about all we have discussed, try and write some words which could be used as an invitation to the table at a service in your church.

Engaging Children

Invite the children who are part of the church congregation to a simple meal, which in itself will give them a sense of belonging. Ask them about special meals that they have been part of. What was it that made them special?

Then ask them what they know of meals that Jesus had with people – be ready to tell some of the stories – and what they know about the Lord's Supper and the way it is shared in their church. This would then be an opportunity to explore and explain why the Lord's Supper is a special meal.

Study Three
Around the Table Today

We have thought so far about the various meals which Jesus shared with disciples and crowds, including the Last Supper. We have also considered the particular situation at Corinth when the church met together around a table. Now we must turn to those occasions, normally as part of a church service, when we gather around the Lord's Table together. How do we understand what we are doing and what do we think God is doing? Central to these questions will be the words we use, words that have not always been easy to understand.

The titles we give

One of the first things we realise is that communion has been described with many different titles, with different parts of the Church having their own preferences. This array of titles itself tells us something about the different aspects of communion. 'Breaking of bread', for example, reminds us of all the shared meals of Jesus and the vital social aspect of eating together, as well as being a reference to Jesus' encounter with the two disciples on the road to Emmaus. The 'Lord's Supper' reminds us that this service does not belong to the Church, but it takes its character and nature from Jesus the friend of sinners. A title often used by other Christians is 'Eucharist', which literally means 'thanksgiving', and reminds us that at the heart of all we do around the table is to offer our thanks to God for all that God has done in Christ. Then 'Communion' itself reflects the two dimensions of fellowship with the Lord and with each other which we expect to experience in sharing bread and wine.

Ordinance or sacrament

Another pair of words involved in the language we use about communion are ordinance and sacrament. At one time 'ordinance' would have been the overwhelming choice amongst Baptists in a reaction against the perceived understanding of sacraments in other parts of the Church. It was clearly the response to the command (ordinance) of Jesus 'Do this in remembrance of me' so often carved upon Communion tables. Over the years there has been less unease over the use of the word 'sacrament'. Baptists have learned to value symbols and the use of our imagination in the things of the faith. A sacrament takes ordinary things, bread and wine, and gives them a new context and meaning. Not only do we witness God's provision for our daily need in ordinary bread, but the wine points to joy in all those things that are not essential to life but add to its fullness. But wheat has to be ground and grapes pressed. In these are symbols of a broken and crushed world offered to God for his healing and acceptance. And this he does in the broken and crushed Jesus.

An important underlying issue in these various titles, and brought into focus in the terms ordinance and sacrament, are the roles that God and the believers play during a service of communion. Ordinance tends to stress our role in being obedient to what Jesus commanded, and remembering him. A sacrament, on the other hand, is often thought of as a 'means of grace', an occasion when God meets with us and offers us grace. The Latin word *sacramentum* was used of the Roman soldier's pledge of allegiance to his emperor and so some then see that at the table, in thanksgiving to the God who first loved us, we renew our pledge of loyalty offered in baptism.

The understanding of the roles of God and the believer has fluctuated amongst Baptists through the centuries. We might think of a spectrum with God at one end and those sharing communion at the other. There have been times in our history where we have stressed very strongly the human end of the spectrum. We have proclaimed the grace of God in offering us salvation in Jesus Christ, but communion is a moment when we remember what God has done in Jesus. Often this was in reaction to other Christian traditions who wanted to stress the (sacramental) action of God in communion offering grace and so played down the role of those coming to communion. There would

> **Communion not only remembers the death of Christ, it celebrates the presence of the risen Christ amongst his people by the Spirit**

be much agreement today that we need to find some interplay between God and us at communion. It is a moment of remembering God's great saving act in the past in Jesus Christ, but also a moment of encounter where we find God's grace offered to us again in the here and now. Communion not only remembers the death of Christ, it celebrates the presence of the risen Christ amongst his people by the Spirit. This will have some influence on who we think should be welcomed at the table. What do we demand of the person who comes, and what do we expect God to offer?

The words we use

A service of communion will usually include a number of familiar words and phrases. Even churches that do not use written prayers or orders of service will repeat again and again words taken from the Biblical account of the Last Supper: 'This is my body; do this in remembrance of me'. However the meaning of words is not always straightforward, and in everyday language we use words in a variety of ways. Before we look at some of these specific phrases, it would be helpful to remind us of several ways words are used.

Words clearly can have a straightforward meaning. When working in the garden you might talk about a rock that is there, or when out for a walk point to the field of sheep. You are thinking of a literal rock and literal sheep. However, in another context, you might use the same words in a less literal and more 'pictorial' way, as indeed the Bible does.

In familiar words, Isaiah says that 'all we like sheep have gone astray.' (Isaiah 53:6) Isaiah does not mean we are literally sheep, but in the same way that sheep have the reputation for wandering off, so we have wandered away from God. We call this way of talking a *simile*.

Alternatively the Bible describes God as a rock (Deuteronomy 32:4 for example). It does not mean that God is an inert lump of some kind of stone. Rather, a rock is a strong and reliable foundation, and so is God for our lives. We call this a *metaphor*.

Such ways of using language, which we do frequently – we might tell someone they are a star – may help us think about some of the more difficult New Testament words we use at communion.

'This is my body which is (broken) for you'.
Baptists have understood this as a metaphor. Jesus' words are full of truth, but

we understand the word 'is' in the same kind of way as 'God is a rock' or 'you are a star' in the sentences above. So at communion the words *'This is my body'* take us to the heart of the mystery of the cross in which Jesus' body is broken for the sins of the world. Words which often accompany the sharing of the bread taken from 1 Corinthians 10:16-17 take the idea of body further. *'The bread which we break, is it not a sharing in the body of Christ? Because there is one bread, we who are many are one body, for we all partake of the one bread.'* The Church is the Body of Christ, the people in whom God's love is shown and lived. To be confronted with the broken bread is to be asked, 'I love you this much. How much do you love me?'

'This cup is the new covenant sealed by my blood.' 'Drink this and remember Christ's blood was shed for you, and be thankful.'
Profound biblical themes resonate here, which take us back into the Old Testament, for example to Jeremiah 31:31-4, as well as to Jesus' last supper. One way we might begin to explain them is to say 'Jesus gave his life for you, now you belong to him and to each other when you welcome him into your life. He helps you to live and love other people as he did. He lives in you.' This is emphasised in our Baptist churches by the common practice of eating the bread as we receive it as a symbol of emphasising that the gospel is for each one of us. And the wine is drunk together as a sign of our belonging together.

'Do this in memory of me'.
Memory here is a lot more than recalling an event long ago in history. I may remember from my school days that in 1453 the Turks captured Constantinople. But that is a very different thing from my remembering my parents and the home in which I grew up and came to faith. Then, deep emotions of gratitude, thankfulness and a sense of an unpayable debt are stirred into life and new resolution formed. When we remember Jesus' death we are remembering a real historical event, but one which has profoundly shaped our lives. We remember too the risen Christ present in the world through his Spirit. So it is that as we remember in communion we experience the love of God afresh and it touches our life in the present. We rejoice again in the joy of the gospel and let it transform our lives in the friendship we extend and the sacrifices we are prepared to make. The past becomes present reality.

'You proclaim the Lord's death until he comes'.
This is Paul's comment and is an essential part of our observance of the Lord's

Supper. Past event and present experience combine together to point us to the future when all humankind and all creation are made new in the Kingdom of God. The promised heavenly banquet also shapes the way that we think and act in the present. This suggests that communion is a kind of preaching, and we will want to reflect on what communion, and the way it is conducted might 'say'.

The actions we make

Communion is of course not only, or even primarily, about words, but interwoven with the words used are certain actions. The person presiding will do certain things, and those who participate will do other things. These actions have meaning in that they form a crucial part of the proclamation which communion makes. From early on as children we have learnt by doing things, often by imitating what we see others doing, whether in play or in a deliberate learning context. The actions we perform in communion continue to shape the people we are and are becoming. We might also think of communion as a visible drama in which the preaching of salvation is acted out. The practical and visible aspects of communion therefore matter, for what we see will be part of the message. It will be important then to think through all the practicalities, not because there is one 'right' way of doing things, but because the practical things, the bread and cups we use, the way everything is arranged, will speak about the gospel. There are various actions which may happen in some services and not others, such as sharing the peace, but at the heart of communion are four actions which copy the pattern of Jesus: taking bread, thanking God, breaking the bread and sharing the bread.

> From early on as children we have learnt by doing things

The President

The person presiding at the table – leading the service – will normally take the bread and after a prayer of thanksgiving will lift it up and break it in front of the congregation. 'This is my body'. We are reminding ourselves that Jesus' body was broken for us on the cross. Even with the custom of having small cubes of bread for the congregation to take, (see below), there will still normally be one larger piece that could be broken. Often when a whole loaf is used it is cut almost through, perhaps into quarters. This makes it easier for the person leading to break the bread and put it on four different plates. But, on the other hand, there is something both more dramatic and more real about having to tear a whole loaf – it speaks more vividly about the tearing of Jesus' body.

In some churches the person presiding will also pour out wine from a jug into a large cup or chalice; in others the wine may already be poured out. Either way mention may be made, drawing on Luke's account of the Last Supper, of the cup that is poured out, symbolising in the same way as the bread the self-giving of Jesus on the cross.

The Participants

Baptists frequently take individual pieces of bread and individual glasses of wine at communion. We did not always do so. Early on in Baptist history there would have been one loaf and a common cup that was shared by the congregation, with all the symbolism this entails of being the one Body of Christ. When the late Victorians 'discovered' hygiene, many of our congregations thought that it would be more hygienic not to tear pieces of bread from a common loaf and not to drink from a common cup. Indeed, makers of individual communion glasses advertised the hygienic properties of their wares! Some of our older churches still have the common cups and plates from earlier days when hygiene was not a consideration.

The individual pieces of bread and individual cups soon attracted another (more 'spiritual') explanation. We eat the bread separately to show that we receive Christ individually; we drink the wine together to show our communion in Christ. However, in all traditions, the bread is eaten individually. Where there is a common cup, the wine is also taken individually – nobody hands out straws for sipping together! Communion is expressed by sharing the cup.

If communion 'preaches', what do cut pieces of bread and individual wine glasses, with their suggestions of a private or individual meal, say as opposed to a common loaf and cup?

The things we repeat

One significant aspect about sharing communion is that it is deliberately repetitive. In our churches we might experiment with new ways of sharing communion from time to time – an Easter Morning Communion around breakfast, for example, or as part of a Maundy Thursday meal – but often communion will follow a very familiar form. Things that are repeated simply out of tradition with no understanding of what we are doing become meaningless, but there is a real and valuable place for the repetition of meaningful and familiar words and actions, which is what we are doing when we share communion. The word 'ritual' is commonly associated with the former – meaningless tradition – but is actually a more accurate description of the latter, the meaningful reliving of familiar words and actions. This is helpful for all of us, but can be particularly helpful for children, as they help build both a sense of identity and sense of belonging as part of the community. We never need to shy away from repeating familiar words and actions, recognising with communion that we will never plumb the depths of meaning in Jesus' death and resurrection, but recognising the way that the familiar can help in developing our understanding and our faith.

Conclusion

All that we have looked at in this study could be focused in the question, 'What happens during communion?'

What do we expect of those who come to the table: baptism, faith, understanding, holy lives, a searching for God?

What do we expect of God when we come to the table: grace, forgiveness, peace?

What do we think that we are doing when we come and repeat familiar words and actions: remembering Jesus' death, remembering moments in our past when we have encountered God, creating and building new memories?

For study and discussion

- Describe what 'normally' happens at communion in your church. Are there aspects of the service where you have been uncertain about their meaning or importance? You might want to draw a quick floor plan of how the church is set out during communion – are there things that strike you about it?

- Have you ever celebrated communion in a very different way, perhaps in your own church in an early morning Easter service, in a housegroup or somewhere else? Describe the differences. Were there aspects of these different approaches that you found more or less helpful?

- Initially communion seemed to be celebrated as part of a meal (this was a cause of the conflict in Corinth we looked at in the previous study) before it developed into a separate act of worship. Do you think there are any advantages or disadvantages to celebrating communion either as part of a meal or as an act of worship?

- The reflection above talks about communion as an ordinance and a sacrament. Is this language that you are familiar with and do these words speak to you in different ways? What have you learnt about other words that describe communion? Which do you prefer and why?

- The reflection also talked about the way we understand the role of God and the role of the believer in communion? What do you think you are doing when you come to communion and what do you expect of God?

- 'This is my body'. Try and write a sentence that describes what this means. (If you doing this as a group, write your sentences on your own and then compare them.)

- 'Do this in memory of me'. If someone new to church asked you what this meant, how would you reply?

- If you were organising a communion service, how would you want to do it? Think about where it would be, the way the place would look, other practical things, who would be involved, what would be said and done....

- In the last study we looked at some words of invitation which might be used at a communion service. In different ways they tried to describe who might come to communion. Drawing on these three studies, and thinking about the different meals of Jesus, Paul's writing to the Corinthians and our understanding of communion, list those things which you think we should expect of, and look for in, those who come to the table for communion. The conclusion above lists some possibilities.

Engaging children

Show a video clip - chapter 28 of the DVD - from the Disney Pixar film 'Ratatouille' – the power of food to bring back memories. In the clip, as the food critic eats the ratatouille he remembers his childhood and the ratatouille his mum made for him.

Invite the children to think about what they have seen. Use the following questions as prompts:

I wonder if certain foods bring back memories for us (be prepared to give examples).
I wonder what memories the food at the Passover meal with Jesus made them remember (be prepared to tell or remind the children of the Exodus story).
I wonder what Jesus meant when he broke the bread and said, 'Eat this bread in remembrance of me'.
I wonder what people remember as they eat bread and wine at communion.
I wonder why churches celebrate communion so often.

Study Four
Children and the Church

In the previous studies we have asked what we think happens as we meet around the table and what should be expected of those who participate. This is necessary for any discussion of what happens with children and communion. But a second way into the question is to begin with children and consider the child's journey in Christian faith and their belonging to the life of the church.

Of course, two conclusions to the question, 'Who can share the bread and the wine?' would make this section either superfluous or rather different. First, if one concludes that the communion table should be open to all - that it is a celebration of the openness of God's kingdom in which there are no boundaries - we do not need to ponder any further on the possibilities of a child's relationship with God to see that they will also be included in the open invitation. Secondly, if one reaches the conclusion that only the baptised should be invited to participate fully in the meal, within a Baptist setting, the question becomes, 'Who can be baptised?' and not 'Who can take communion?' We will then be thinking about children in the context of a different (although obviously connected) question.

The contemporary practice of most of our Baptist churches suggests that some limits are placed on the invitation to the table, but that the limit is not defined by baptism. Whereas once communion was limited to the baptised members of the church, often happening after the service, the invitation to, and location within the service of, communion is now open to any who believe and love the Lord Jesus. This is not to imply that baptism is no longer important – our hope for our children must be that one day they come to be baptised – but we do not make it a requirement to be welcome at the table. We therefore need to reflect carefully on the nature of a child's relationship with God in order to decide whether or not a child may be invited to participate in communion. Children are now much more frequently present during communion, whereas in our past this part of the service was restricted to adults. So we need to consider the presence of all children at communion, and how their presence might be affirmed and welcomed. In this study we begin to wrestle with the first of these questions.

There are two important aspects to this question of boundaries: faith and the Body of Christ. If participation in communion is primarily about a person's faith-relationship with Christ, how do we discern the capacity of a child to enter into relationship with Christ? If taking the bread and wine is about belonging to the Body of Christ, where do children stand in their relationship to the church? This study explores some of these questions about a child, their relationship with God and how children belong in the church.

Jesus and children

The Gospel accounts of Jesus ask deep and searching questions about our attitude to children, both in society and in the church. He was keen for children to be both seen and heard. He was angered by the attitude of his disciples who tried to prevent parents bringing their children to Jesus. They failed to recognise that his openness to people on the margins of society extended to children as well as to lepers, tax-collectors and prostitutes. "It is to such as these that the kingdom of God belongs", Jesus told them (Mk 10:13-15).

When the disciples wanted to know about greatness, Jesus made a child centre-stage: "Whoever becomes humble like this child is the greatest in the kingdom of heaven" (Matt 18:1-4). In the temple, after Jesus' entry into Jerusalem, Matthew tells how the chief priests and scribes were angered by the children's cries of, "Hosanna to the Son of David!" Jesus, on the other hand, welcomes the children's praises (Matt 21:14-16).

Jesus cuts through the cultural expectations of his time, indeed the social norms of so many societies. Judaism, relatively speaking, gave children more dignity than many surrounding cultures. Nevertheless, Jesus challenged even them by affirming the place of children in the embrace of God and in the life of the kingdom. He confronted attitudes that treated children as inferior or left them on the outside until the day when they would cross the threshold into adulthood. Furthermore, children became a focus for Jesus' teaching about discipleship. Where the disciples might have expected Jesus to tell children that they needed to grow to a mature faith in God, Jesus took the opportunity to tell the disciples that whoever does not receive the kingdom of God as a little child will never enter it.

When his disciples argued about being great he told them, "Whoever welcomes one such child in my name welcomes me, and whoever welcomes me welcomes not me but the one who sent me". (Lk 9:48)

Where adults are called upon to be role-models for children, Jesus calls upon adults to discover the way of discipleship by learning from children. Where children are expected to catch glimpses of the divine in adults, Jesus invites his followers to give time to children, because to welcome a child is to welcome the presence of God in our midst.

Children in gospel communities

What will be the characteristics of communities that allow their life to be informed and shaped by these Gospel stories? This has more to do with the quality of the community's life, than its institutional structures. If Jesus brought children from the margin to the centre, then a community that is true to Jesus will be willing to welcome children into the heart of its common life. Jesus challenged the prevailing practice and culture both for the sake of the children and for the sake of the adults. Children needed to be embraced, touched and blessed, no less than others. Equally, adults need to engage with children in order to tap into that rich vein of human experience that is characteristic of childhood. When children are kept to the margins both they and adults suffer.

> a community that is true to Jesus will be willing to welcome children into the heart of its common life

When these Gospel narratives resonate in the life of a fellowship a new dynamic between children and adults will emerge. Space will be opened for a genuine mutuality, in which children learn and grow through their encounter with adults, and in which adults similarly learn and grow through their encounter with children. If children need constantly to be stretched towards a maturity of faith, adults also need to learn that way of faith which Jesus describes as 'becoming like a child'. Such faith is learned not in theory nor in contemplation, but through encounter with the childlike.

Towards the middle of the last century the traditional Sunday School pattern was questioned. The questions came out of a desire to be truly gospel communities where children are not on the margins, but are welcomed into the centre of the church community. Some began to see that the Sunday School was perhaps not the best way of integrating children into the life of the church. It met at a different time to the rest of the congregation (on a Sunday afternoon). It usually met in a different building (often next door, but sometimes over the street). Its main emphasis was teaching and learning and not worshipping. The church was certainly investing a lot of time in its work with children, but children were not really being welcomed into the heart of the church's life. And so the move to 'Family Church' or 'Junior Church' took place. Typically, children joined in for the first fifteen or twenty minutes of the morning worship with the whole congregation and then went out to their classes. For some churches, everyone would be considering the same theme from different perspectives each week. Admittedly, there were churches for whom the move from afternoon Sunday School to morning Junior Church was a purely pragmatic response to falling numbers and a declining number of available Sunday School teachers. However, for many there was a desire to bring children much more fully into the heart of the worshipping life of the church.

The closing decades of the twentieth century saw churches continuing to work at learning to be gospel communities with our children. Some felt that although Sunday School had moved from the afternoon to the morning, children were still being treated as add-ons to the main community of the church. They were still there to learn from the adults. The adults were not encouraged to interact with the children and gain from the interaction. The participation of children in the worship life of the church was still felt to be limited. They were, in large part, still absent from the focal points of worship. New ventures in all-age worship, like 'Messy Church', have appeared in recent years that are

> Any discussion on the place of the child in the Christian community will seek to value the child as a whole human person

about children and adults worshipping together. Alongside this, researchers are revealing insights into the spirituality of children, and the ways in which we can think of children growing and developing in expressions of faith appropriate for the child. It is also becoming increasingly apparent how children are able to respond to symbolism in worship – the candle that is brought forward at the beginning of worship as a sign of God's presence; the holding of hands as a sign of the church as family. (As Baptists we would do well to pay more attention to symbols as a means of helping children (and adults!) to locate themselves in worship).

Valuing the child, valuing childhood

Any discussion on the place of the child in the Christian community will seek to value the child as a whole human person, but will also seek to value childhood itself. We do our children no favours when we introduce them to experiences before they are ready. There is a careful balance to be found in giving dignity to children and recognising their full capacities, while protecting them from experiences and responsibilities that would harm them.

It is right, for instance, that children now are allowed a healthy interest in their bodies, and that questions such as "Where did I come from, Mummy?" are answered in an open and honest way. An appropriate openness about sexuality is far better than the evasiveness of a previous generation. However, the over-sexualised culture in which our children grow and develop is far from healthy.

Within the spiritual life of the child, we meet the same challenge. How do we respond to the spirituality and faith of children in the church, without requiring that they take on adult responsibilities sooner than is healthy for their development and growth? Some things in the past have been thought inappropriate for children because children's full potential has not been realised. However, there will be occasions when the caution of the past is grounded in wisdom. Valuing the child in the child's relationship with God will be to value childhood's expression of faith as valuable in its own right. In order to be of value, the child will not simply imitate the adult.

A Charter for Children and the Church

One product of the thinking about the place of the child in the church which developed at the end of the twentieth century is the Charter for Children and the Church. It originated in the Church of Scotland and the United Reformed Church. The question we might ponder is whether this contains a vision of what a church might be like that takes Jesus' attitude to children seriously.

1 Children are equal partners with adults in the life of the church.
2 The full diet of Christian worship is for children as well as adults.
3 Learning is for the whole church, adults as well as children.
4 Fellowship is for all – each belonging meaningfully to the rest.
5 Service is for children to give, as well as adults.
6 The call to evangelism comes to all God's people of whatever age.
7 The Holy Spirit speaks powerfully through children as well as adults.
8 The discovery and development of gifts in children and adults is a key function of the church.
9 As a church community we must learn to do only those things in separate age groups which we cannot in all conscience do together.
10 The concept of the 'priesthood of all believers' includes children.

Conclusion

This study has raised questions about the role of children in our churches by reflecting both on the way that Jesus interacted with children and the history of our churches over the last century. It raises important questions for us.

How have our churches changed, and have they done so with clear intentions and understanding or for very pragmatic reasons?

What understanding do we have of children in relationship to God and the church and how is that portrayed in what we do?

For study and discussion

- Hymns from either end of the twentieth century betray different approaches to children's involvement in the life of the church. Compare the following two hymns. What are their different emphases? Read them in the light of the Gospel passages. How do they reflect a gospel concern for children? Which most reflects your own church's attitude to children?

Christ who welcomed little children
to thine arms in Galilee,
lovingly we greet this baby
that *she* too be blessed by thee.

Lord, accept the parents' praises
help them by thy grace divine;
may their tender care and nurture
train and lead them to be thine.

In their home may thine own presence
guide and guard from day to day,
filling life with love and gladness
throughout all *her* childhood's way.

Then in strength of mind and body
may she own thee Lord and King,
tread the paths of Christian service,
all *her* heart's allegiance bring.

Christ who welcomes little children
bid this baby welcome too.
May thy mighty arms protect her
all life's varied journey through.

Hugh Martin 1890-1964

The child among us is a gift,
to treasure and enfold:
a child declares the love of God
embracing young and old.

The child among us is a way
to see the face of God:
when we receive the smallest one
we meet our cross-marked Lord.

The child among us is a sign
of how we are to be:
a people of the reign of God,
of trust and liberty.

The child among us is a guest
with us, at Christ's high feast:
with bread and wine we all are fed
and sent to serve the least.

The child among us is a pledge
of what is soon to come:
a world of justice, hope and joy,
in Christ, in us, begun.

© Michael McCoy, South Africa

- Think further about the role of children in your own church. Can you trace or research the history of the last 50-60 years and plot a time line with significant changes in Sunday worship, midweek activities, etc which involve children? Then, when you come up to date, how would you describe the place of children in your church?

- When children come to church now, they are used to learning in school in very different ways from the way we adults learned in our schooldays. Society also sees children very differently from the time when 'little boys and girls should be seen and not heard'. In what ways has your church changed to reflect these wider developments? What might be the important changes still to make?

- The reflection above suggests that important changes were made for the benefit of adults as well as children. Look back on your time line and think again about the way your church has changed. List ways you think that the adults have benefited from the different ways that children are now included in church.

- Read Mark 10:13-15. What do these verses have to say about both adults and children in your church? What might you need to do as a church to take seriously what Jesus said?

- Read Matthew 18:1-4. What do these verses have to say about both adults and children in your church? What might you need to do as a church to take seriously what Jesus said?

- New Testament scholars tell us that the rabbis called their disciples (learners) 'children' and 'little ones'. Jesus might have had this in mind too. If so what might this say about all of us, young and old, being learners together, and how we should care for each other?

- Read again the 'Charter for Children'. What do you find helpful about this charter? What do you find unhelpful?

- If your church implemented this, how would your church change? Would it be healthy for the development of the children?

Engaging children

Read Mark 10:13-15. Invite the children to think about what they've heard. Use the following questions as prompts to imagine themselves in the scene.

I wonder why the disciples did not want the children to be there.
I wonder why Jesus was cross with them.
I wonder what Jesus said to the children who were there.
I wonder how the children felt.

Study Five
Children and Faith

Below is an extract taken from one of the services for infant presentation in *Gathering for Worship*, the most recent book of patterns and prayers from the Baptist Union of Great Britain.

Church Promises

Do you, the members and friends of this church,
promise that there will always
be a place for children here
and that you will play your part
in bringing our children to a knowledge of Jesus Christ
as their own Lord and Saviour?
If you do promise this, then please stand.

Family Promises

Do you thank God for the Gift of A
and do you trust God
to help you as parents
as you care for *her/him*?

We do.

Will you try, with God's help,
to share with *A* your understanding of Christian faith?

We will.

Will you bring *her/him* up within the community of the church?

We will.

Blessing

The minister receives the child, may lay a hand on the child's head, and says

A, you are one of God's children
and your name is written in the palm of God's hand.
The blessing of God,
who is Father, Son and Holy Spirit,
be with you today and always. Amen.

Welcome

*After the blessing of the child, the children of the church may offer a sign of
welcome to the child. This may be the gift of a children's Bible, or, as below,
a candle. A representative of the church, perhaps a child or a member of the
junior church staff, may say*
A, I give you this candle
to remind you that Jesus is the light of the world.
May you grow in his light and, one day,
shine for him.

This simple liturgy makes, or implies, a number of significant things about the child,
the family and the congregation.

First, and perhaps most significantly, the order of service declares that the child is
already a child of God. Any understanding of us as human beings, at any age, must
take some account of a Christian understanding of sin and the fall, but this subject
is acutely raised in connection with young children. The service above claims that
all children begin life included in God's grace and their names are written in the
palm of God's hand. The God who wills all to be saved, and who gives particular
concern to the vulnerable, holds all children in loving grace. This is not to suggest
that children are innocent or sinless, but alongside acknowledging children are
bound to sin (by which we mean they are born into a humanity defined by sin and
that they will sin), they are not outside the grace of God.

Secondly, alongside this statement of God's grace, there is also the strong sense that the child being welcomed and blessed is on a journey, not just in life, but also in faith. This is most clearly stated in the poetic language of the welcome, in the hope that the child may grow in the light of Jesus and one day shine for him. This then is the context for asking the parents whether they will share their understanding of the Christian faith with their child – to help them on this journey of faith.

Then, thirdly, it is clear from the questions and promises that the responsibility for helping this child on her or his own journey of faith is shared both by the parents and wider family, and also by the 'family' of the church. Will there always be 'a place for children here and will you play your part in bringing our children to a knowledge of Jesus Christ as their own Lord and Saviour'?

These three assumptions or beliefs expressed in this moment, often near the very beginning of a child's life, clearly fit together to offer us an insight into how we should understand the place of children in our church. It suggests a starting point as God's child, a journey of faith leading to personal commitment, but continuing in a life of witness and service, encouraged and helped along the way by both family and the wider church community. The children in our church are on the way of faith and we are seeking to help them. One of the Biblical passages often read at an infant presentation is Deuteronomy 6:4-7, which includes the command: 'Keep these words that I am commanding you today in your heart. Recite them to your children and talk about them when you are at home and when you are away, when you lie down and when you rise.' Faith is not something anyone invents, but is something received – 'handed on' (1 Cor 11:23;15.3) – through the worship and life of the church.

But how do we understand children 'being on the way' and their own particular faith development, and how can we as local congregations best help them? These are the questions we will explore further in this study.

Children and faith development

Many years ago John Locke (1632-1704) proposed the notion that children were empty vessels or blank slates. Although it is still sometimes heard today, it is an understanding that has unequivocally been disproved. The view of the child amongst those in education today is of the child as a competent learner from birth – they have skills, knowledge and understanding which they bring to the learning process. They are not passive learners, but active participants contributing to the community's learning.

In recent years there has been a lot of research into children's spirituality and faith development. What this research has reminded us is that children are spiritual beings and can have real faith. Children reveal an openness to the world, to feelings, to other people, and to God, which adults often seem to lack. They express a curiosity which leads them to ask questions, both simple and profound, to explore and wonder about the world, other people and God, in ways which adults often seem to lose. We therefore value the faith of children for what it is, appropriate to their stage in their journey. Integral to such an approach is an understanding of the work of the Holy Spirit in the lives of children. If we understand that a child is a child of God, we can expect God to be working in the life of that child through the Spirit in many and varied ways. Although there have been various ways that a particular work of the Spirit has been linked to a moment of 'conversion', baptism and filling with the Spirit, there has also been the understanding that the Spirit is at work bringing all people, whether adults or children, to a deeper faith and trust in God. We can therefore expect to see God's Spirit gently at work in the lives of our children as they are opened to the faith of the congregation in scripture, in song and in prayer.

> **Children reveal an openness to the world, to feelings, to other people, and to God which adults often seem to lack**

If we insist that the sign of faith is only the ability to verbalise, we separate it from action – how we treat one another, how we live gospel lives. An emphasis on faith as something predominantly verbal will often dismiss the faith of children (and perhaps also many adults). Children's faith may not be expressed or articulated in the same way as an adult's, but it will be appropriate to their age or experience of God's love, and should be respected, accepted, nurtured and encouraged on that basis. The word 'faith' is very hard to define and is used in different ways. At one level we might say it means simply to 'trust', but we also use it as a noun to distinguish Christian beliefs, those things as Christians we understand and confess. There is also a suggestion that we should understand faith as a verb, as a journey which a person is on. For children, then, we both respect and nurture their journey and also rejoice with the gift that the child is to the family and that he or she brings to the church community.

Children, then, are on their own journey of faith, but how does this relate to their status in the church? For those churches which practise infant baptism, this rite offers a clear boundary when children are considered part of the church. As Baptists, insisting that baptism is for believers only, we have therefore often struggled both to articulate our understanding of the place of children and to develop appropriate practices. Yet the passing on of faith from one generation to another is of great significance. While the church must engage in wide mission to include families with no church background and connection, there is also this very specific need, which is becoming ever more challenging, to be passing on our faith to the children who are growing up within our congregations.

If we understand children – especially those within families who are committed to the life of the congregation – as very much part of the family of the church, then we must see a child's development and growth within this context. Some Baptists have argued that children (especially those who have been part of the church from an early age) are on a journey not only *towards* faith, but also *within* faith. Many of our children, in the same way as many adults, would not be able to pinpoint a moment when they started to believe; rather they have always grown up with that faith. In fact some would argue that this should be the expectation for our children who grow up in church. Several conversations between Baptists and other Christian communions in recent years have stressed that 'initiation', or beginning the Christian life, is not a one-point event but a kind of process or journey. For Baptists, a service of infant presentation can stand near the beginning of this journey, and emphasise that the children involved are part of the covenant community of the church, received into the love and nurture of the church family.

> Some Baptists have argued that children are on a journey not only towards faith, but also within faith

This would have implications for our understanding of baptism. For those who have grown up within the faith who come to baptism, this is not a boundary marker in the sense of either moving from no faith to faith, or from being outside the church family to moving inside. Rather we must view it as a significant milestone on the journey, when a person publicly makes the faith of their family and their church their own, declares their commitment to this journey of faith being a life-long commitment, and pledges their willingness to take up the serious responsibilities of serving in God's mission in the world. At the same time, in baptism they receive gifts of the Holy Spirit to enable them to share in God's mission as an active disciple. This in turn may influence decisions about the age of baptism. The question moves from being "Does this child have faith?" – for this has already been affirmed and valued – to "Is this person ready to make the faith they have grown up in their own as a life-long commitment? Are they ready to take up the cross as a disciple, serving others in the world?" Baptism will then be linked more closely with church membership and the ability to be actively involved in church life and ministry in the world as a disciple of Christ.

A congregation and faith development

Given all that we have said about a child being on a journey *within* faith we must ask how that journey is best nurtured and developed. Clearly family, both immediate and extended, have a crucial role to play. But within our services of blessing and dedication we have also recognised that it is not simply the responsibility of each family, but the wider congregation has a significant role in the nurture of their children. Faith is never purely an individual, or even a family affair; it is something genuinely corporate.

In recognising that faith is shared by and in the community, there has been a desire from some voices to recover the ancient description of 'catechesis'. This was the process by which people were discipled into the Christian faith. This was more than a ten-week course, but was a long process of being transformed and formed by the faith and witness of the church. Central to this process was being a part of the community – participation in the regular occasions of worship and fellowship, of mission and action, were integral to this gradual process of development. We need to discover means of discipling through experience, reflection, commitment and action. Our aim in providing children with age-appropriate groups and including them in worship is to see them experience the faith of the church and come to own that way of life for themselves. As Baptists we perhaps have more to do in order to nurture young missionary disciples.

Such an understanding of spiritual development is mirrored in the fields of both child development and adult learning. One of the ways in which we all learn is through imitation and participation, which in children is seen most clearly both in shared tasks between adult and children (eg cooking together) and also in play, in which by imitating patterns of behaviour (eg actions and speech) we make sense of the world around us. As well as cops and robbers, doctors and nurses, and teacher and pupils, you may see children playing church: "I'll be the minister, you can be the congregation". By imitating as well as participating, children and adults learn. We might want to ask what it is children observe or experience in the life of the church that they might imitate.

So if being part of the congregation is important for the faith development of children and others, where they can participate and experience, and be active and involved, we may need to reflect on whether our current practices as a local church enable this to happen. The move to experiment in all age worship and in inter-generational learning is part of a response to this. And in this context of worship we come again to the question of communion. This, it could be argued, is a key moment of participation and experience where the family of the church gather together. Drawing again on the roots of the Last Supper in the Jewish Passover, this was one of a number of significant and repeated occasions when all the Jewish community would share in moments that shaped faith and enabled and encouraged the youngest members of the community to grow into the faith of the community.

As Baptists, where we hope our children are on the way to baptism, is participating in all aspects of worship, including communion, an important way of enabling them to learn and grow and encounter God? Does it help them on the way, where exclusion might damage their sense of belonging and growth?

What faith, then, might be 'necessary' for participation? Certainly not the faith of an adult, but rather the faith appropriate for the age of the child, for whom the experience is a genuinely spiritual one. This is a question to be followed up in the final study.

Conclusion

This study has explored the ways that children can be participants in the worshipping life of the church as children. It has suggested that this is good for the church, but also vital for the faith development of children, that they might grow in faith to the point of baptism and then on to fuller maturity. The challenge for each local church is to envisage how this might be best worked out in its own context.

For study and discussion

- Look back at the extract from the order of service at the beginning of this study. What strikes you as important in it? Are there aspects of it that you would like to change or omit? Are there things you would like to add? (You might like to find a copy of the whole service in *Gathering for Worship*, alongside other such services in that book and elsewhere.)

- How do you view children? What adjectives might you use?

- What words or images do you associate with 'faith'? In what ways have you experienced the faith development of children, perhaps as a child yourself, through your own children, or others in the church?

- If participating in communion requires faith, what kind of faith does it require and how do we best judge if that faith is present?

- The previous two studies suggest that children are a gift. What do you think children in your church have to offer to the church community? How might the church receive and welcome this?

- The study suggests we all learn by participation and by active involvement. In what ways are children in your church able to participate and be involved and how might this be developed?

- If children learn by participation, might participating in communion be a helpful or unhelpful way for them to grow in their faith? How might they be able to participate in a way that treats them seriously as children but not yet as adults?

Engaging children

Make a simple dice with the following pictures on different sides: bread, wine, Bible, people, praying hands and the word 'remember'.

Introduce the game by talking about communion, depending on how much they have experienced and the practice of the church.

Play a game in which the children roll the dice – can they say something about the picture facing up when it lands? (Other pictures could be used to explore other things, eg baptism.)

Study Six
Children around the Table

We have looked in the previous studies at various aspects of communion and also the changing understanding of children and their faith development. In this last study we will look at some of the practical alternatives, which have been tried by different churches, shaped by the different theological issues we have identified. The conviction of those preparing the material is that children have a very real place in church life, and that there could be some occasions when children are present for communion – that the whole of the church 'family' join together. It is also our conviction that children should be taught about communion, and need to be present at times for this teaching to be real. But what part might children play?

In trying to come to your own decision it is better to proceed slowly and carry opinion with you than to impose a practice with which many may be unhappy. It is also important for a Local Ecumenical Partnership to be sensitive to its members' traditions and to consult them before adopting a new practice. Formal permission may be required from them and from the Regional Sponsoring Body. We recognise as well that within our churches will be people who themselves have grown up in different Christian traditions and there will always need to be some sensitivity shown here.

Theological factors

Studies four and five explored the nature of children, as we encounter them in the Gospel and as they develop in faith. The conclusion is that we should treat children as children and not as adults. This might sound rather simplistic, but is actually much more profound. Children are part of the church and can develop in their faith and their relationship with God, but they do so as children not yet as adults. Recognising both the importance of children in the Gospels as models of receiving the Kingdom, and the centrality of communion as one of the highlights of our worship experience together, some churches have found a place for children to be welcomed and included at communion. But it is important that we expect them to act as children rather than as adults. This is about valuing childhood while still taking children seriously. There is often some concern that if children are present and part of communion, they will not know how to behave or be reverent enough; but while we should not expect adult behaviour, we do know from experience that children understand the need for quietness and stillness and that they can act appropriately.

The first three studies looked at the nature of communion and several important themes emerged that have relevance for this practical question about children and communion.

communion is an interplay of grace and faith

We saw that communion is an interplay of grace and faith. It is a celebration of God's self-giving grace in Jesus, which evokes our response in faith. But what kind of faith is necessary? In particular do we also assume a certain understanding and maturity when we talk about faith, and is the concern that children do not understand enough? In this interplay between grace and faith, is the simple desire to know God and God's love enough? What will be crucial is that in the interplay of grace and faith for children, the faith we look for is the faith of a child not an adult.

We have also thought about the way that communion might confirm and strengthen faith, particularly when it is viewed as something that follows baptism. But, in addition, we began to explore the way that communion might also nurture faith, perhaps quite a young and embryonic faith, so that this faith grows and develops into maturity. In this scenario baptism may come later partly because gathering round the table has shaped and nurtured faith. Some may be concerned that baptism is downplayed by children taking communion, and so is seen to be unimportant and might disappear. An alternative way to look at it is to see that those who participate in communion, whose faith is being nurtured at the table, are either building on their baptism or are on the way to baptism. Clearly there is no definite commitment, but we see this theologically as a journey in which baptism will be a notable highpoint.

Practical possibilities

Churches are already developing different ways of responding to the request of children to be included in communion. Here are six models which might be explored. They are based on different theological commitments and conclusions from the previous studies, so it will be important to think through the reasons for each model. But all six have in common the presupposition that it is important for children to be present sometimes at communion, and to have some participation, for example by receiving a blessing.

Model 1

Participation in communion should follow baptism and church membership, meaning that all those, including adults, who participate would need to be baptised. Children are encouraged to show their discipleship to Jesus by patiently waiting until they are able to express their relationship to God as Jesus did. Children are encouraged to wait not because they are children but because it is believed that a public confession of faith should precede their sharing. Up until this point children might be encouraged and welcomed to communion, but to receive a blessing rather than bread and wine.

Model 2

Participation in communion does not need to wait until after baptism but should follow on from a clear sense of 'conversion', in which the child decides to follow Jesus for themselves. Discussions with the minister or church leaders would confirm that any particular child is in a position to take communion, which becomes in some way a public confession of faith.

Model 3

Children are invited to share in communion if they have been previously blessed in a service of 'Presentation of Children', if they can testify to some kind of simple faith in Christ (appropriate for their age and development), and if they are receiving Christian teaching with baptism as the aim in the future (even if this is likely to be as much as ten years ahead). The point of having received 'infant blessing' is that they do not come to the table as individuals, but as those who have been welcomed into the covenantal life of the church by the congregation. If they have not received a blessing when they were very young, they can be blessed and the church can pray for them some short time before sharing in the table. While not yet baptised, they are 'on the way' to baptism, and so the link between the two events is not lost. This model fits into the insights about 'catachesis' developed in the last session.

Model 4

All children are welcome, and they are encouraged to reflect on whether they love Jesus and want to follow him. Parents, or those who bring them, are responsible for their children and decide with them whether they should take the bread and wine. They are seen as part of the church family and are an important part of the church's life. Communion is sometimes celebrated in small groups of about eight in the context of the whole.

Model 5

Children participate in the communion service, but rather than share bread and wine, they receive symbols of promise, recognising that they are part of the wider church community but not yet fully members. This may be grapes (not yet made into wine) or milk and honey – Old Testament signs of promise. This could happen at particular festivals, such as Christmas, Easter, Pentecost, Church Anniversary, and children could remain with their parents or church friends. No minimum age is expected and the extent to which they participate is left to the parents and their children to decide.

Model 6

Drawing on the view that the meal is a gracious invitation to all, children are free to receive the bread and the wine as they wish. Communion can then become a moment of encounter with God in Christ, perhaps for the first time. All are included in until they opt out. Experience shows that younger children do join in but opt out in their teens and then participate again as they grow in faith and join the church. The words of invitation may then be altered from 'all who love the Lord Jesus Christ', to 'all who wish to receive Christ's love'.

Making decisions

First we might ask the question *how* we decide, given all the different variations and the significant theological considerations involved. One way would be to go through the models listed above thinking carefully about each one. The following questions might help:

a) What are the advantages and disadvantages of this model?
b) What does this model say about the nature and meaning of communion?
c) What does this model say about God?
d) To what extent would the children feel included or excluded in this model?

e) Does this model help the adults and the children to learn from one another?

f) Does this model help or hinder faith development?

g) How happy would you be to practise this model with your congregation?

It may be that one of the models seems to be right for your church, or it may be that you develop some combination or something quite different.

Then we might ask *who* should decide. At the very beginning of our studies we told the story of our family faced with an immediate decision to be made. We may not like to be in that position of having to make an instant response, and hopefully these studies has helped to think through the issues so that a more considered answer can be given. But this story placed responsibility with the parents. In one of the models above, this is made explicit, and parents or guardians should always retain an important role. But there is also the need for the church as a whole community to think through the issues and reach a common mind. This is an instance when the Church Meeting can be at its very best, reflecting carefully on Scripture and holding together the pastoral concerns of different members. Hopefully these studies will offer resources for churches as they seek to find this common mind.

> We want to treat children as children but still as important and significant members of the church family

Conclusion

These studies have sought to give resources to help think through both the real nature of communion and the place of children in our church. We want to treat children as children, but still as important and significant members of the church family, who have much to give as well as receive. We also want to treat communion seriously as an important moment when the congregation together meets with the risen Christ around his table. In the midst of these issues, we also recognise that local churches will need to make guidelines for how they will both encourage children to act and also respond to questions raised, and that these guidelines will vary from church to church. But we hope that these studies have been helpful in this process. In the final chapter we offer some resources for how some of these ideas might be lived out and celebrated in our worship around the table.

For study and discussion

- Look at each of the six models suggested and go through each carefully, asking the six questions listed above. Look back over your discussions and answers for the first five studies which will help you tackle the questions, and keep a note of your thoughts and responses for each model.

- Are there other models which you think might also work in your particular situation?

- From these studies and your reflections on the models above, what would you suggest might be an appropriate way for children to be present at communion in your church, whether on a regular basis or on special occasions?

- However or whenever it takes place, should the moment when we first take communion be marked in a special way? Discuss the possibilities and opportunities created by such an occasion.

Engaging children

Explain all or some of the models listed above to a group of children and ask them for their reactions and their feelings. Which ones do they like?

Resources for Worship

The challenge we face is not only to think through biblically and theologically questions about children around the table, but then to reflect on the way that our worship includes children and others in such a way that all can grow in their discipleship.

Here we offer some worship resources which offer creative ways of recognising all ages present in worship. They do not assume one particular model discussed in chapter six, but they have been written on the basis that there are some moments, whether regular or occasional, when children are present when communion is celebrated.

Some resources are offered here which pay attention to different parts of what happens and is involved in communion and which offer some examples of possible words and actions. All these examples are taken from the experience of those who have prepared this study.

Other resources for sharing communion are available, and in particular Baptist ministers Clare McBeath and Tim Presswood provide lots of possibilities at:
http://dancingscarecrow.org.uk/Dancing_Scarecrow/Eucharists.html

1 Preparing the table

Communion will, of course, not just happen – it will have been prepared for not only by bringing bread and wine, but in how the church is set out and in the wider worship of the service. All these elements of preparation can help explore and explain the meaning and significance of the Lord's Supper to all people and in ways that are particularly helpful for children.

a) The layout of some Baptist churches is fixed but many are very flexible. So where is the table placed – at the front, off to one side, in the middle of the church? We often use language about gathering around the table, even though we do not physically do it. We tell the story of a meal but a service of communion appears to be quite different. Thinking about the way that the physical and the visual connect with the spoken will help all those learning about faith and being formed within the community. Having the table physically in the centre, for example, so that the congregation sit round it means that communion becomes the focus of worship.

b) The pattern of a service is very flexible. A traditional and helpful pattern has been for communion to come at the end of the service – its climax, saving the best till last – after the ministry of the word through scripture and a sermon. Such a pattern might work well when communion is celebrated as part of an all-age service or where the pattern is for the whole congregation to be together at the end of the service. But if children are to be in groups for teaching, and leave part way through, it might be best to celebrate communion at the beginning of the service before the children will move to their groups. This can suggest that being the family of God and sharing the family meal is the most important thing we do.

c) There is also scope for reflecting on and developing the way the table is physically prepared. While it has been traditional in many Baptist churches for the table to be set before the service and covered with a white cloth, there are many more creative possibilities. The covering of the bread and wine itself sends out a message that some are not welcomed, and this needs some rethinking. And rather than have the table already set there is scope for quite powerful symbolic actions as bread and wine are brought forward. This can be accompanied by or follow on from other symbols such as a Bible, a cross and a candle. Children, as well as others, appreciate both the visual and also the repeated – theology enacted in the symbolic which they know and gradually understand at a deeper level. The table may be set through the service, perhaps beginning with a candle for Jesus' presence as the light of life, adding a Bible as the Word is read, the cross after a prayer of confession and the bread and wine. Although it takes some preparation and timing, involving the children of the church in making some bread, for example as part of thinking about the feeding of the 5000, which is then brought in for communion is very powerful. Setting the table can be a significant and powerful way of beginning to tell the story.

> being the family of God and sharing the family meal is the most important thing we do

2 An invitation

The celebration of the Lord's Supper will normally include an invitation to gather around the table (which does not normally mean moving but recognising what is going to happen) and to participate. This offers a means of explaining what is happening and the story the table tells. There are rich opportunities here to enable children to begin to be drawn into the meaning of the Supper.

a) Using questions and answers to explain what is happening (based around the pattern of the Passover):
    One of the children of the church asks the questions and the answers may be given by either one person (eg the Minister) or the whole congregation:

Question:	Who are we remembering and who is here with us?
Answer:	Jesus Christ, our Lord and Saviour who lives today.
Question:	Why do we break and eat bread?
Answer:	To show that Jesus' body was given up to death for us.
Question:	Why do we take and drink wine?
Answer:	To show that Jesus shed his blood for our sins.
Question:	Why is there one loaf and one cup?
Answer:	Because we are one family; we belong to each other because we belong to Jesus.
Question:	For how long will Christians celebrate like this?
Answer:	Until Jesus comes again in glory.

b) Children are invited to help act out the drama

    In an all-age service on Palm Sunday, which on that occasion did not include communion, three different scenes were played out in the midst of and with the congregation (the focus of each scene was in a different place in the building), who were invited to enter into the story in different ways. These scenes were the entry into Jerusalem, the Last Supper, and the denial of Peter.

Before the service a table was set with a tablecloth, a loaf of bread and a cup of juice in the middle of the congregation. When the second scene is played out the service leader walks to the table and invites a number of children, who had been pre-warned, to come and sit at the table. The service leader reads Mark 14:17-25 (preferably having learnt it) and at the appropriate moments the service leader breaks the bread and offers it to the children around the table and takes the cup and drinks from it. The whole congregation is invited to reflect on what it might have felt like to have been invited to that first table. In the same way they are invited to reflect on what it might have felt like to be at the entry into Jerusalem and in the courtyard with Peter.

c) An invitation using straightforward words is used regularly and repeatedly so all the congregation can grow in understanding the implications of the words:

We gather at this table to celebrate life:
The life of God in the world,
The life of God in Jesus,
We come to break bread and pour wine,
We come to tell the story of Jesus again,
We come to be forgiven,
We come to be renewed in faith,
We will eat and drink,
We will receive words of promise,
We will be blessed,
For God is one who loves to bless.

3 Telling the Story

At the heart of Baptist approaches to the Lord's Supper is telling again the story of the Last Supper, of that night when Jesus was betrayed. Traditionally Baptist worship has not included this in a prayer of thanksgiving, as for example in most Anglican worship, but has been a narrative told to the congregation again. Often the story has been told by the reading of those verses from one of the Gospels or from 1 Corinthians 11, but this can be added to in other ways.

a) Where quite young children at present, it might be appropriate to draw on the style of the CBeebies programme *Something Special!* In this programme the children have to look for special things. In communion we are wanting to say bread and wine are special things. *Something Special* also includes a lot of sign language and children with special needs, so the prayer of thanksgiving with sign language (below) would be appropriate to follow this.

On the night Jesus was arrested,
he gave his disciples a loaf of bread and a cup of wine
and said they were something special.
So when you see the bread and the cup
wave and cheer because they are Jesus' special things.

Where is the bread, can you see it?
> *Bread is brought forward*

Where is the cup, can you see it?
> *Cup is brought forward*

A loaf of bread and a cup of wine
some of Jesus' special things
to remember him,
to trust in him
and to be loved by him.

b) The story could be told by the congregation.
Echoing the practice of Passover used in section 2 (above) a child asks:
'Tell me the story of this meal'.
One adult (warned in advance) could tell the story of the Last Supper in their own words.

Or the story could be told by different members of the congregation, with one person beginning the story and others in turn adding something further until the story is told. This then becomes something like a version of the game 'when I went to the supermarket I bought …'.

4 Prayer of Thanksgiving

A celebration of the Lord's Supper will also include a prayer of thanksgiving in some form. It might be appropriate to attend to the question of when this happens in the church year. In Lent it might lend to a quieter, more reflective communion, while in Easter it might lend to a noisier, more celebratory communion. The different seasons have different moods which can help children grasp that communion is a meal where we remember that Jesus died and yet also a meal where we celebrate that Jesus is alive.

a) Using simple sign language for the prayer of thanksgiving
Jesus thank you for the world
Jesus thank you for this church
Jesus thank you for this day
Jesus thank you for saving us
Jesus thank you for the Holy Spirit
Jesus thank you this bread and this wine
Jesus we love you

b) Using a simple song
Thank you Jesus (Anon)

or

Here is bread, here is wine (Graham Kendrick, © 1991 Make Way Music)

c) A responsive prayer of thanksgiving for Easter:
This table celebrates Jesus
who died but was raised to new life.

This table celebrates Jesus
who died but was raised to new life
with bread and with wine.

This table celebrates Jesus
who died but was raised to new life
with bread and with wine
with thanksgiving and worship.

This table celebrates Jesus
who died but was raised to new life
with bread and with wine
with thanksgiving and worship
with running feet and shouts of joy.

This table celebrates Jesus
who died but was raised to new life
with bread and with wine
with thanksgiving and worship
with running feet and shouts of joy
with humble hearts and open hands.

5 Sharing the Peace

This is an element which is not always present in Baptist celebrations of communion, but which offers another opportunity for enacted theology as the central theme of reconciliation is expressed. Extra care needs to be taken to make sure this is appropriate and welcoming, not embarrassing!

a) If words which express God's peace are regularly said as part of communion, then on occasion these could be spoken by one of the younger members of the congregation. This would be very much in line with the Gospel story, as long as the congregation resist any temptation to clap but rather recognise that through this child they are hearing words from God.

b) Invite two members of the congregation to form a human sculpture. They kneel facing one another, heads resting on each other's shoulders, hands on one another's upper arms in the style of the statue of reconciliation by Josefina de Vasconcellos (which can be seen at Coventry Catherdral). This becomes a visual symbol of peace that the communion meal enacts. (This idea comes from a chapter by Sam Wells in *Faithfulness and Fortitude* (T & T Clark, 2000), p132).

c) If there is a smaller congregation, perhaps as part of a particular occasion such as Maundy Thursday or Easter Sunday then words of peace can be offered and expressed by giving everyone a candle, lighting the first one from a central candle and then that person lighting the next person's candle with the words' God's peace be with you', and so until all candles have been lit.

6 Sharing Bread and Wine

Depending on which of the models from Study 6 is used then children will participate in different ways at this point. The Baptist practice has tended to be for people to remain seated and be served, which can be developed or re-thought.

a) When children are welcomed to participate fully in receiving bread and wine then there may be times when children are among those who serve the bread and wine to others. Being part of communion on a regular basis is a formative experience and children will quickly pick up the way that they should do this from what others have done on previous occasions, and can serve with sensitivity and dignity. Again this echoes the Gospel narrative of putting children in the middle as an example.

b) When the children are welcomed into the part of the service but with the expectation that this is not yet the moment for them to receive bread and wine then the congregation can be invited to come up to receive communion. It can allow a practice of families being together with children receiving a blessing or grapes and biscuits. This can also allow children the freedom to move, rather than having to remain sitting quietly. It can also set up formative patterns of making a response and can help children, as well as others, understand that as Jesus comes to us, so we come to him.

The Apostle Paul said

"I received from the Lord what I also passed on to you".
It is with joy we seek to pass it on to others.